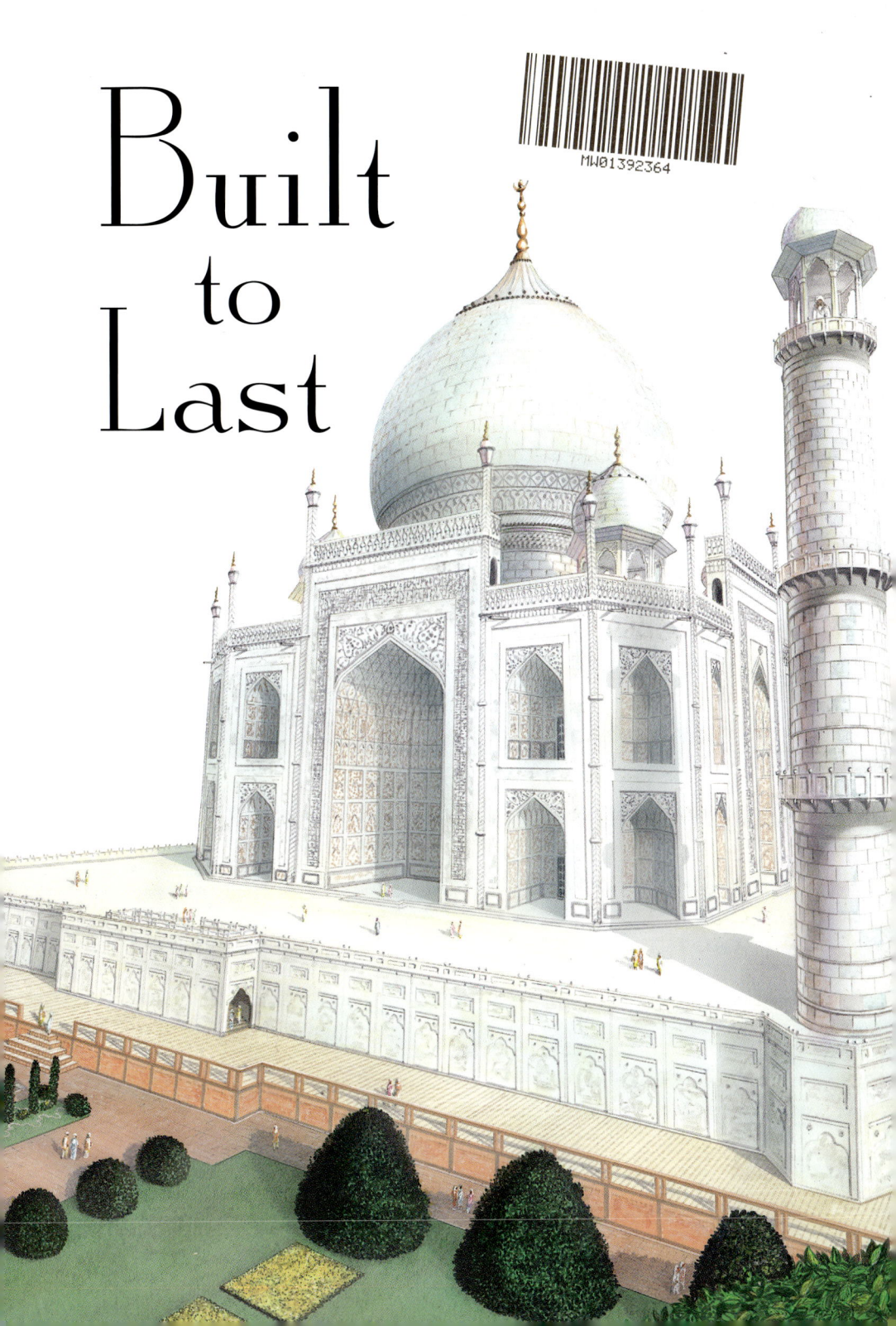

Built to Last

Contents

A Leaning Legend	4
The Art of Building	6
Amazing Architecture	
In Search of Order	8
Built for Harmony	10
Balance and Beauty	12
Eye on Europe	14
A Little of This . . .	15
Brave New Shapes	20
Reaching for the Sky	24
Hard Hats, Please!	26
Cold Comfort	28
Glossary	30
Index	31
Research Starters	32

Features

Who invented concrete? How did they make it? Find out in **Making Concrete** on page 9.

There is a famous building in India called the Taj Mahal. To find out what the words *Taj Mahal* mean, turn to page 12.

You may know of this person as a painter or sculptor, but he was also a famous architect. Read **The Greatest Dome in Rome!** on page 18 to learn more.

Would you pay money to sleep on a bed of snow in a room built of ice? Check out two very chilly hotels in **Cold Comfort** on page 28.

How do building designs keep sports fans happy?

Visit **www.rigbyinfoquest.com** for more about BUILDINGS.

A Leaning Legend

IN FOCUS

Come to see the world's most famous building that went wrong—the amazing leaning Tower of Pisa. Other towers stand straight and tall, but the bell tower of Pisa leans 14.5 feet to one side!

Then join a tour of some of the most interesting buildings in the world.

This architectural wonder is a must-see in Italy. The leaning Tower of Pisa is one of the best!

Leaning Tower of Pisa Tours, Mon.–Fri.

Italy

Tower History

The building of this decorative bell tower began in 1173 and, after many stops and starts, was finished between 1360 and 1370. In the first year of construction, after only three stories had been built, the architect realized his bell tower was leaning. The weight of the building was causing the unstable soil beneath it to sink. The construction of the tower was continued, with a few changes that were hoped to correct the tower's lean. Nothing, however, could stop the tower from sinking.

Tower Workshop

Kids, come and make your very own leaning tower.

Workshop open daily 9:00 A.M. to 1:00 P.M.

Materials provided

The Art of Building

The most simple buildings provide people with shelter. However, the art of building, or **architecture**, achieves much more. Many people around the world have spent their lives designing and working on buildings for people to live in, work in, learn in, play in, and relax in. Some of these buildings are amazing works of art and engineering. Some are very old. Others are new.

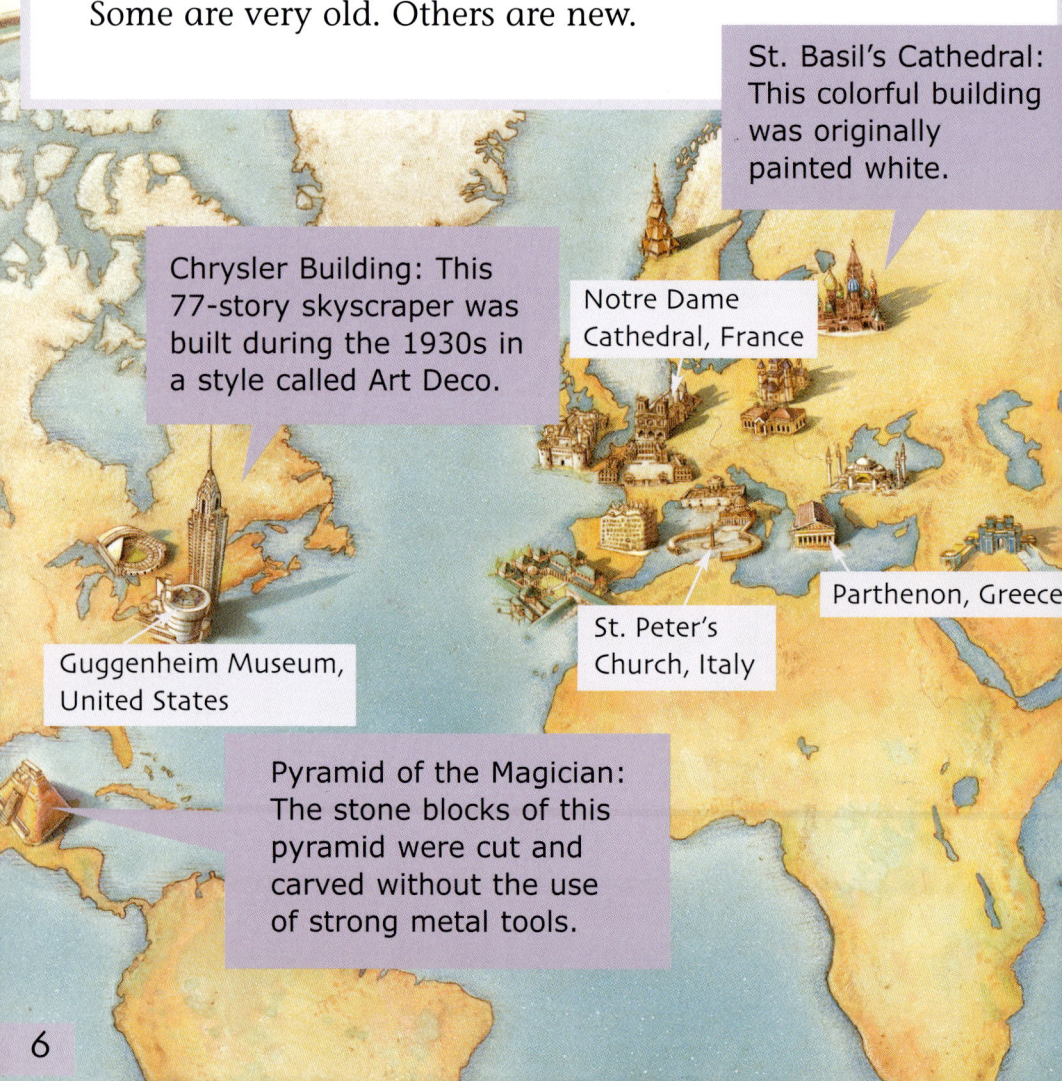

St. Basil's Cathedral: This colorful building was originally painted white.

Chrysler Building: This 77-story skyscraper was built during the 1930s in a style called Art Deco.

Notre Dame Cathedral, France

Parthenon, Greece

Guggenheim Museum, United States

St. Peter's Church, Italy

Pyramid of the Magician: The stone blocks of this pyramid were cut and carved without the use of strong metal tools.

A great building can show many different ideas and styles. It can also tell us about the beliefs and values of the people who designed it, built it, and used it, both in the past and today. The pictures on this map show just some of the world's great buildings. There are many others.

Hall of Supreme Harmony, China

Horyuji Temples: These temples were built 1,300 years ago. Today, they are the oldest wooden buildings in the world.

Taj Mahal, India

Kandariya Mahadeo Temple: More than 1,000 carved figures cover this 1,000-year-old temple.

Sydney Opera House, Australia

Amazing Architecture

In Search of Order

As long as 2,500 years ago, the ancient Greeks built many magnificent buildings. They believed that a building should be balanced, or in proportion, with doors, roofs, windows, and decorations blending together neatly. Their buildings were often made of white marble, and the roofs were supported by columns. Greek architects used math to make sure everything was balanced and orderly. The ruins of these ancient buildings still stand today.

In nearby Italy, Roman architects copied the Greeks. However, their cities soon became crowded, and they needed new building styles. Over 2,000 years ago, Roman architects designed the first apartment blocks.

Nearly 2,000 years ago, the Romans used layers of arches to build a huge arena called the Colosseum. Today, thousands of people visit the ruins of the Colosseum every year.

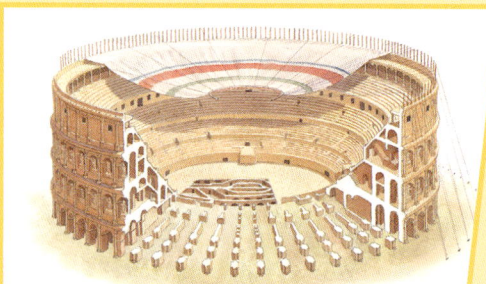

Parthenon, Athens, Greece

TECHTALK

Making Concrete

Roman builders invented concrete by mixing lime, water, volcanic soil, and small rocks or broken bricks. They then poured the concrete between two brick walls. The Romans used this invention to help them make large, strong buildings.

Colosseum, Rome, Italy

SITESEEING · PEOPLE & PLACES

How do building designs keep sports fans happy?

Visit **www.rigbyinfoquest.com**
for more about **BUILDINGS**.

Built for Harmony

A country's architecture often shows the values of its people. In China, **philosophy** and building are closely linked. Both deal with how a person finds his or her place in the universe. For example, a family's house is seen as the center of the family's universe. Similarly, the emperor's palace was seen to mark the center of China and the whole universe.

The ancient Chinese built their important buildings, such as the Hall of Supreme Harmony, on platforms. They thought of the platforms as being like Earth and the roofs of the buildings as being like the heavens, or sky. The roofs are turned up at the ends. This makes them look as if they are floating above the building.

Hall of Supreme Harmony, Beijing, China

Amazing Architecture continued

Crossbeam
Bracket
Short beam
Column

Beams and Brackets

Chinese roofs are often held up by crossbeams instead of walls. The crossbeams rest on short beams that stand on a beam below. This means that only a few columns need to go all the way to the ground, and there is more space in the building. Each column has a pair of "arms" that support the beam above. These arms are called brackets.

Balance and Beauty

The Taj Mahal in India is thought by many people to be the greatest work of architecture. It was built by Shah Jahan, an emperor of India, as both a monument and **mausoleum** for his dead wife, Mumtaz.

One of the reasons the Taj Mahal is very striking is that it is perfectly **symmetrical.** Even the gardens surrounding it are balanced exactly, with canals dividing the gardens into four equal parts.

The Taj Mahal is built entirely of white marble. A 10-mile ramp was laid through Agra so that elephants could drag blocks of marble to the building site. This magnificent building took 22 years to build, and it is thought that about 20,000 people worked on it!

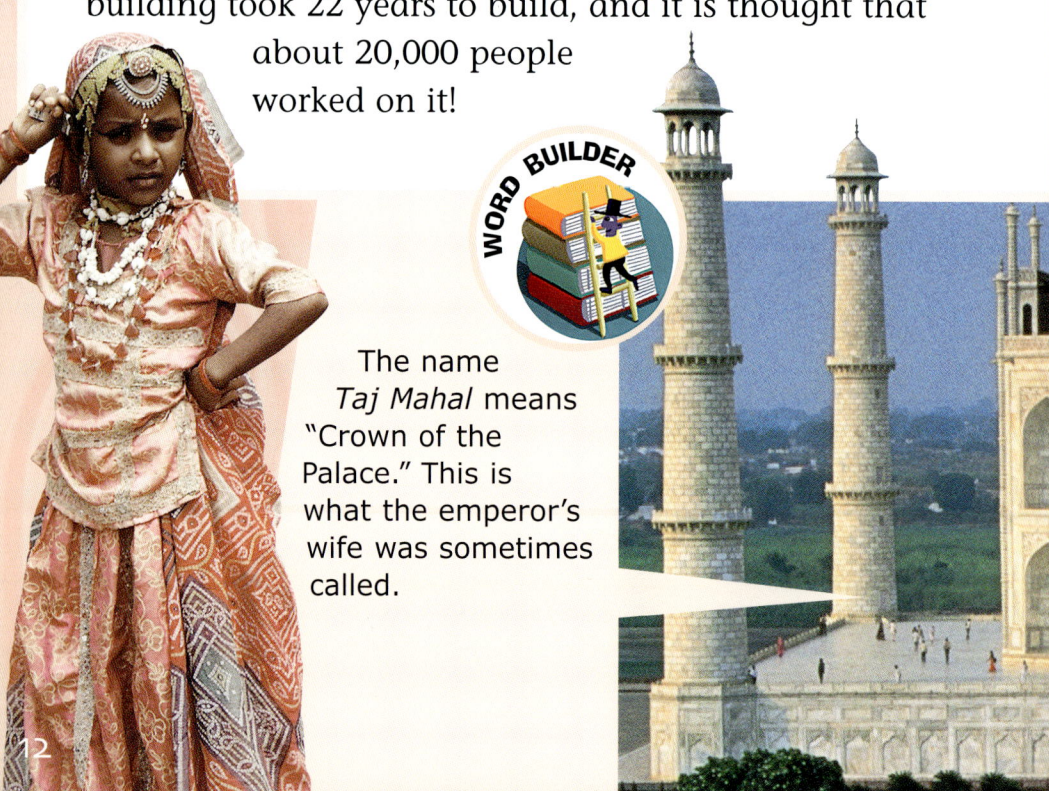

WORD BUILDER

The name *Taj Mahal* means "Crown of the Palace." This is what the emperor's wife was sometimes called.

Amazing Architecture continued

The walls and floor of the Taj Mahal are decorated with beautiful carvings and stone inlays. The inlays are made from 35 types of precious and semiprecious stones.

Taj Mahal, Agra, India

The inside of St. Peter's is designed in the Baroque style. It has many columns, and the floors, walls, and ceilings are highly decorated.

Bramante was the original architect of St. Peter's. He designed the building using square and circular shapes of the Renaissance style.

Bramante's plan

At the top of the dome is a lantern to let in natural light.

A Little of This . . .

St. Peter's Church in Rome, Italy, is a great example of a building that shows different styles of architecture. Eleven architects designed St. Peter's, and three different styles were used: **Renaissance**, **Mannerist**, and **Baroque**. Construction began in 1506 and took more than 100 years to finish.

The front of St. Peter's is designed in the Mannerist style. It has windows and doors in many different sizes and shapes. It is also wider than the church and high enough to partly hide the great dome.

The dome is 140 feet across and stands on legs 250 feet tall. Because there are no supports directly below the dome, it seems to float over the inside of the church.

Eye on Europe

A new style of architecture using different methods of building began in Europe during the 1100s. Architects and **stonemasons** learned how to build higher than before by using pointed arches. They also used stone braces, called flying buttresses, on the outside of the buildings to help support their height. These supports look like decoration, but without them, the stone ceilings would collapse. This highly decorated style of building, complete with carvings of people, animals, and plants, is called Gothic architecture.

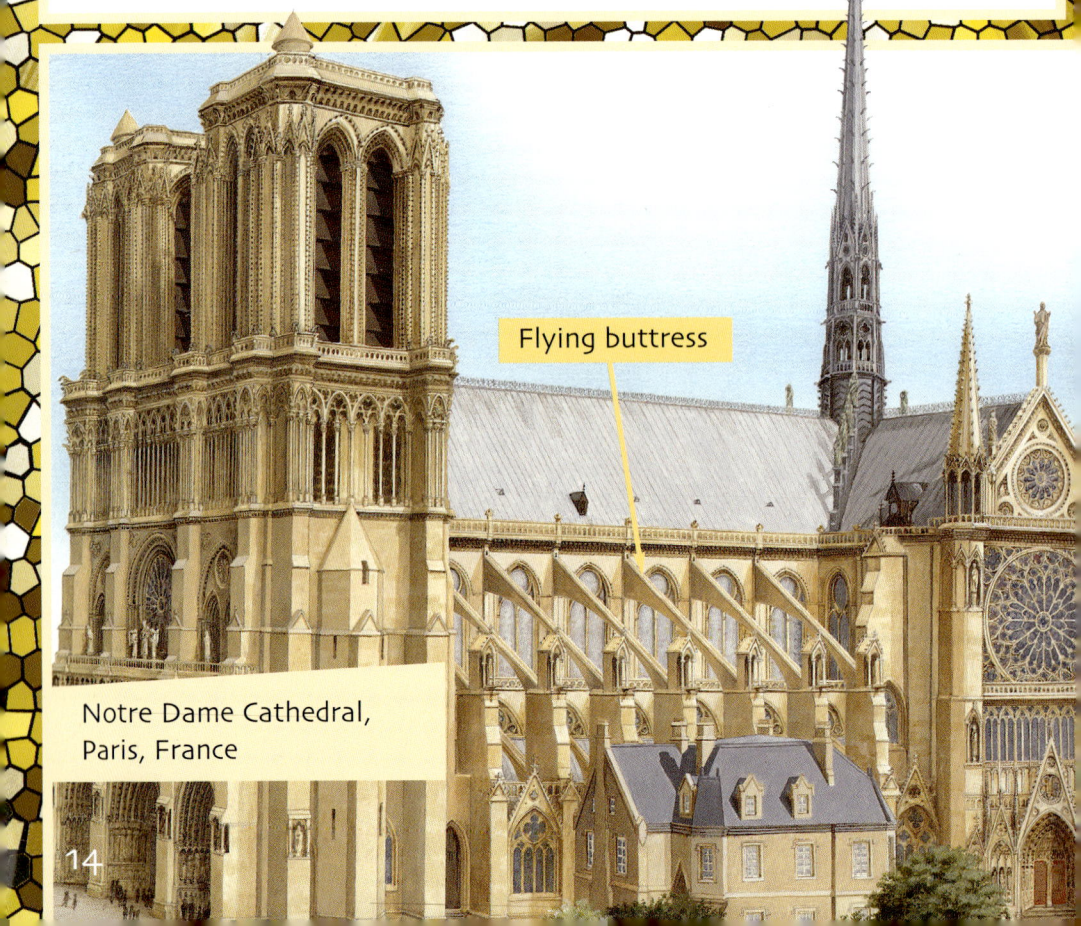

Flying buttress

Notre Dame Cathedral, Paris, France

Oxford University, the oldest university in Britain, is also built in the Gothic style. This can be seen by its many spires that rise into the skyline. A renewed interest in Gothic architecture developed in Britain during the 1700s to mid-1800s. This movement was called the Gothic Revival.

Oxford University, Oxford, England

One of the first and most beautiful Gothic buildings was an important church in France called the Cathedral of Notre Dame. The Cathedral was begun in 1163 and finished about 150 years later.

The Greatest Dome in Rome!

Eye on Europe continued

Michelangelo (1475–1564) from Florence, Italy, was one of the most famous artists in history. He carved many beautiful sculptures and painted many well-known paintings, including the ceiling of an important building in Rome. To paint this huge ceiling, Michelangelo used a technique called fresco. The paint was applied to freshly laid plaster, which means that the pictures are actually painted *into* the ceiling rather than *onto* it. Michelangelo had to work quickly before the plaster dried.

As well as being a sculptor and a painter, Michelangelo was an architect and a poet. In 1546, he was made the head architect of St. Peter's Church. Michelangelo worked on St. Peter's, without pay, until he died in 1564. It was Michelangelo who designed the most outstanding feature of St. Peter's, the dome.

When Michelangelo's frescoes were cleaned in the 1980s, restorers found they had been painted in much brighter colors than previously thought. The brightness of the colors meant that the paintings could be clearly seen from the floor, 70 feet below.

PROFILE

Around 900 workers and 240 horses moved this Egyptian **obelisk** across Rome and then stood it upright in the center of the courtyard, or piazza.

17

Brave New Shapes

Architectural styles grow and develop. Changes in society bring about changes in architecture. After World War II (1939–45), many people were feeling confident and looking forward to the future. The buildings of the 1950s and 1960s reflect this positivity. Many have unusual shapes. This was made possible by the invention of **reinforced concrete.**

When the Guggenheim Foundation decided to build a U.S. museum of modern art in New York City, they wanted a building as exciting as the artworks inside. The architect, Frank Lloyd Wright, designed a building in the shape of a spiral. Some people did not like a building being so different from traditional designs.
Others were excited by the brave new shapes.

Guggenheim Museum, Bilbao, Spain

Instead of moving from room to room, visitors to the Guggenheim Museum in New York walk along a spiral ramp. This means they can see art hung on different levels at the same time.

Guggenheim Museum, New York, United States

Nearly forty years after building the museum in New York, the Guggenheim Foundation built another incredible museum in Bilbao, Spain. The architect, Frank Gehry, designed a wiggly, curving building that looks like a huge sculpture.

In 1957, a Danish architect named Jørn Utzon won a contest to design an opera house in Sydney, Australia. His design included roofs that looked like the sails of boats. The judges loved this fresh, new design. However, the architect, a team of engineers, and computers took several years to figure out a way to actually build it. Sixteen years after the original design was accepted, the Sydney Opera House was completed. Today, it is recognized as one of the most interesting buildings in the world.

The roofs of the Sydney Opera House make it different from any other building. They are made of more than 2,000 concrete sections, held together by 217 miles of steel cable. Over 1 million tiles were used to cover the concrete.

The Sydney Opera House was opened in 1973. During its first twenty years, over 36 million people visited it—that was more than twice the population of Australia during this period. More than 2,500 performances of operas, concerts, and plays are held there every year.

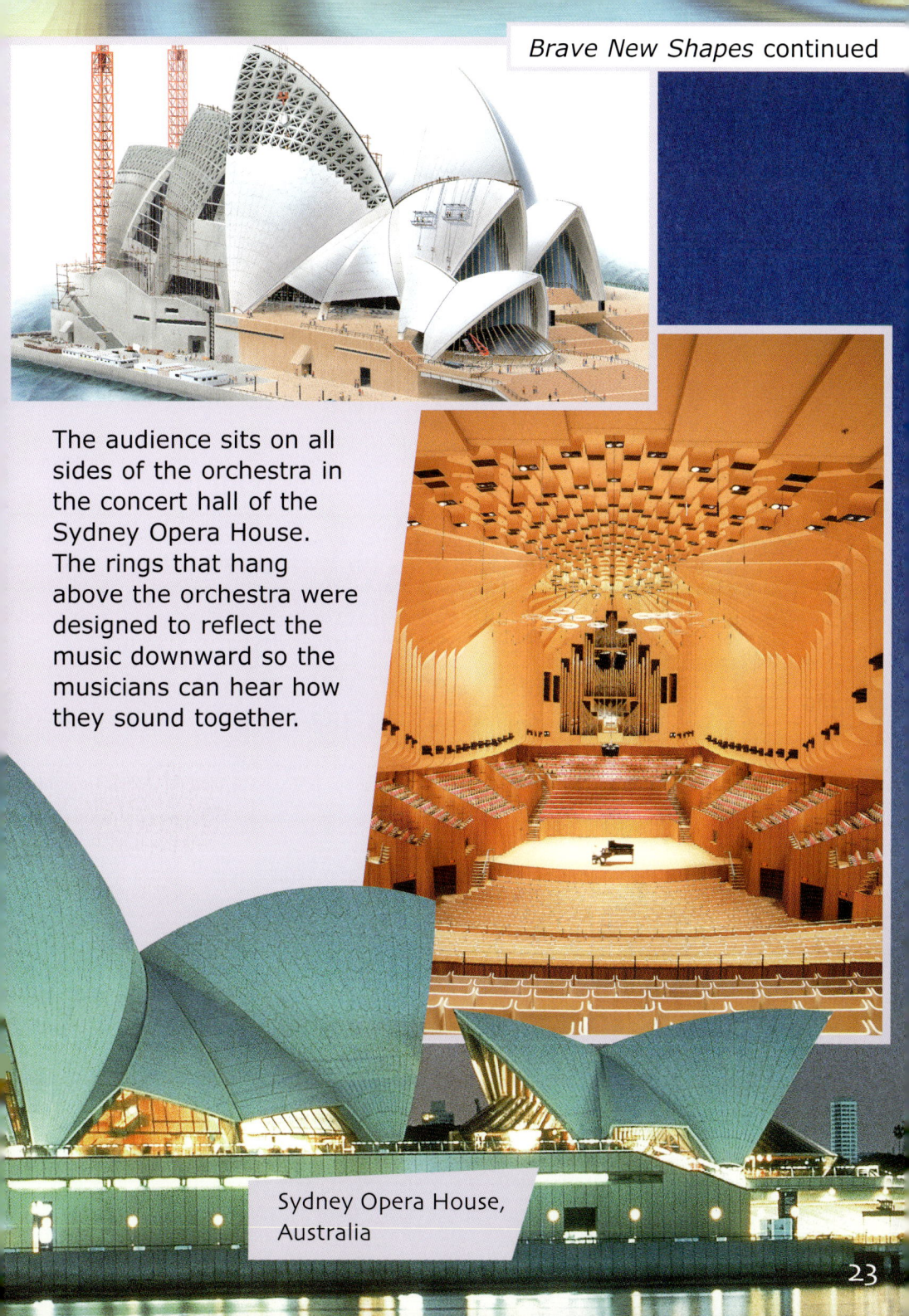

Brave New Shapes continued

The audience sits on all sides of the orchestra in the concert hall of the Sydney Opera House. The rings that hang above the orchestra were designed to reflect the music downward so the musicians can hear how they sound together.

Sydney Opera House, Australia

Reaching for the Sky

Today, some of the world's tallest buildings seem to nearly reach the sky. However, it wasn't until the 1800s when metal frames were first used that very tall buildings could be made. These tall buildings, called skyscrapers, were an answer to overcrowding in cities.

The first skyscraper was built in the U.S. city of Chicago in 1884. It was only 10 stories high. Today's tallest skyscrapers by measurement to the structural top are the Petronas Towers in Kuala Lumpur, Malaysia. They are 88 stories high (1,483 feet).

There are many tall towers in the world. Most of these towers were built for telecommunication. The tallest of them all is the Canadian National (CN) Tower in Toronto, Canada. At its topmost point, the CN Tower is 1,815 feet high.

TECHTALK

Elevators

The first elevator was invented over 2,000 years ago by the Greek mathematician Archimedes, but elevators didn't become common until the 1800s. Before this, the height of buildings was limited by the number of stairs people were able, or willing, to climb. In 1857, an elevator was invented that would not fall if its cable broke. Architects could then build higher than ever before.

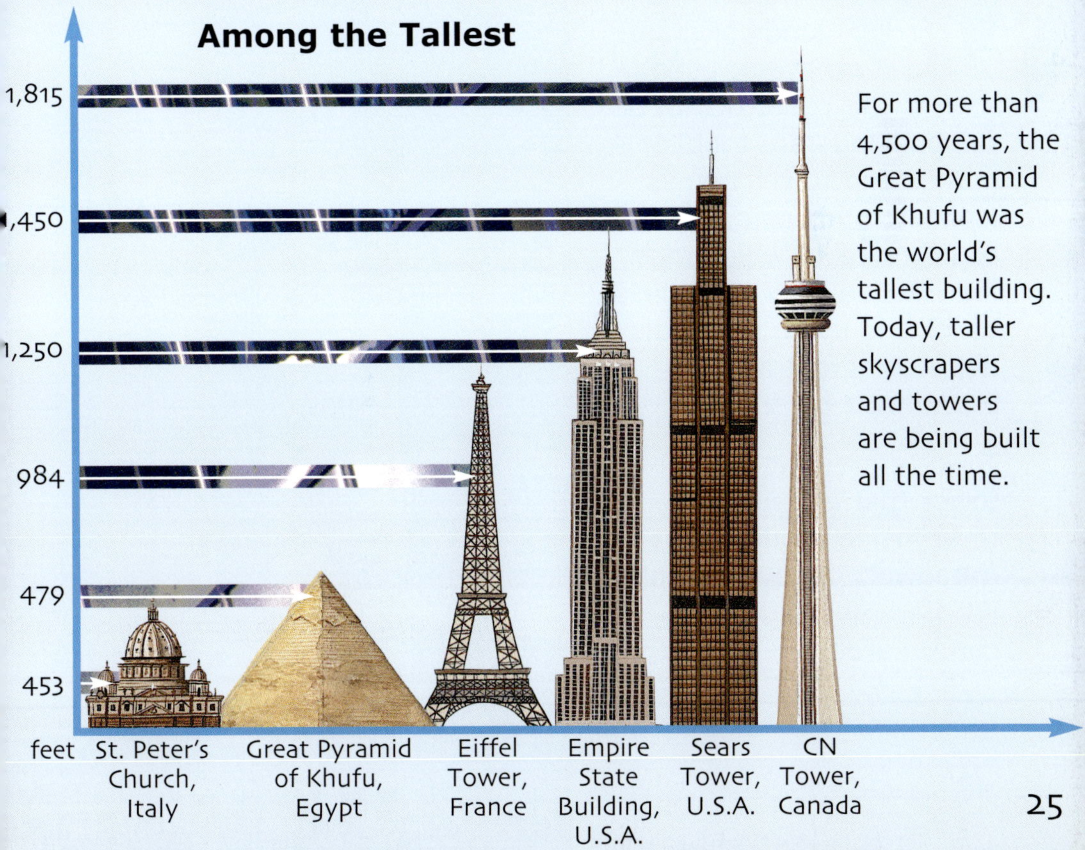

Among the Tallest

Height (feet)	Building
1,815	CN Tower, Canada
1,450	Sears Tower, U.S.A.
1,250	Empire State Building, U.S.A.
984	Eiffel Tower, France
479	Great Pyramid of Khufu, Egypt
453	St. Peter's Church, Italy

For more than 4,500 years, the Great Pyramid of Khufu was the world's tallest building. Today, taller skyscrapers and towers are being built all the time.

Hard Hats, Please!

Since building first began, methods of construction have been constantly improving. The ancient Egyptians had no vehicles, machinery, or iron tools. They cut large limestone blocks with copper chisels and saws. Huge groups of workers dragged the heavy blocks to the building site. The blocks were then dragged up ramps and put into place. This method of construction required huge numbers of workers and many years.

The two main kinds of cranes that are used in the construction of tall buildings are mobile cranes and tower cranes. Mobile cranes can move to any area in which they are needed. They are used to lift and place materials and equipment around a construction site.

Tower cranes sit on a steel tower that is built next to or inside a building's framework. They can only lift materials within a certain area.

With the help of machinery to move, cut, and connect building materials, modern skyscrapers can be built in one or two years. Today, many buildings are partly assembled in factories and then shipped to construction sites. This method, called prefabrication, is quick and economical.

CONSTRUCTION ZONE

HARD HAT AREA

IN FOCUS

Cold Comfort

Most architects design buildings that they hope will stand for a long time. However, the architects of the world's two coolest hotels know that their masterpieces will last only three months before melting into a slushy heap during spring. That might sound like a short life for a building, but the architects get to design a new building every year.

What materials are used to build these hotels? The answer is 10,000 tons of snow and 350 tons of ice. These amazing ice hotels are built every year in Jukkasjärui, Sweden and Quebec, Canada.

Not only are the buildings made of ice but the furniture is ice-cold as well. Guests sleep wrapped in cozy sleeping bags and reindeer skins on beds of snow and ice. Don't worry, there's no chance that the beds will melt. The room temperature is between 16 and 25 degrees Fahrenheit.

Each year at the end of October, architects and builders get busy well before the first guests arrive in mid-December. Machines are used to mold snow over large steel frames. After two days, the snow has frozen into place and the frames are removed. Then, in late November, the builders use tractors and special ice saws to remove huge blocks of ice from rivers. This ice is used to make columns that provide extra support for the hotels.

Sculptors saw and chisel blocks of ice into columns, windows, doors, desks, beds, chairs, tables, lamps, and sculptures.

Glossary

architecture – the art of designing and constructing buildings

Baroque – a style of European architecture during the 1600s and 1700s. Baroque architecture often included huge columns, bold curves, and striking statues.

Mannerist – a style of architecture popular in Italy from about 1520 to 1600. Mannerist architecture used complicated patterns to express the confusion of the times.

mausoleum – a building that contains the burial place of at least one person. Mausoleums are often large and impressive.

obelisk – a stone pillar with four sides and a pointed top

philosophy – the study of the meaning of life, the problems of right and wrong, and why we believe as we do

reinforced concrete – concrete containing steel rods or wire mesh to make it stronger. Almost all large modern buildings have reinforced concrete.

Renaissance – a style of architecture that began in Italy during the early 1300s. Renaissance architecture used simple shapes such as circles, squares, and triangles.

stonemason – a person who cuts, prepares, and builds with stone

symmetrical – having matching parts or shapes on both sides of the center line

Index

architects
- Gehry, Frank — 21
- Michelangelo — 18
- Utzon, Jørn — 22
- Wright, Frank Lloyd — 20

Colosseum — 8–9
concrete — 9, 20, 22
construction — 5, 8–9, 11–12, 14–15, 22, 24, 26–27, 29
elevators — 25
Guggenheim Museum, Spain — 20–21
Guggenheim Museum, United States — 6, 20–21
Hall of Supreme Harmony — 7, 10–11
ice hotels — 28–29
Notre Dame Cathedral — 6, 14, 19
Parthenon — 6, 9
skyscrapers — 24–27
St. Peter's Church, Rome — 6, 15–18, 25
Sydney Opera House — 7, 22–23
Taj Mahal — 7, 12–13
Tower of Pisa — 4–5
towers — 4–5, 24–25

Research Starters

1 Find out about some famous or interesting buildings in your area. When were they built? What style of architecture are they? Who were the architects involved?

2 When the Sydney Opera House was first designed, the technology needed to build it did not exist. Design your own building, including features that require technology of the future to build them. What kinds of technology would be needed? How would it work?

3 Research to find out more about architects. What kind of training do they have? What kinds of architects are there?

4 Different people like different styles of architecture. Find pictures of three different-looking buildings and then interview your family and friends about which style they like best. Display the interview results as a graph.